HEAVEN OR HELL?

YOU DECIDE!

TAKE CONTROL OF YOUR DESTINY!

RELONZO "DELL" RICHARD, SR.

Contents

ACKNOWLEDGMENTS	iii
DEDICATION	vii
FOREWARD	ix
Testimonial of Relonzo "Dell" Richard, Sr.	11
Testimonial of Rico	18
Testimonial of Dennis Parmenter	22
Testimony of Gerald Benoit	23
Testimonial of DeAndre Griffen	26
Testimonial of Charlie K. Jones	35
Testimonial of Greg Thomas (aka) Anthony Pitts	37
Testimonial of Anthony L. Webb	42
Testimonial of Travielle James Craig	44
Testimonial of Greg Sanders	47
Testimonial of Darell L. Flowers	48
Testimonial of Lamarr Cooks	50
Testimonial of Kenneth Underwood	53
Testimonial of Odell Hale, Jr.	55
Testimonial of Brother Maurice	57
Testimonial of Dortell Williams	61
Testimonial of Virgil Clark	64
Testimonial of Maelon Niblett	66
Testimonial of Hamid Zadeh	68
Testimonial of Donald E. Mitchell	72

Testimonial of Hamilton Green   73

Testimonial of Averial Alexander   76

Testimonial of R. Chapman   78

Testimonial of DeAngelo McVay   80

Testimonial of Keith Littlefield   82

Testimonial of G. English   84

Summation   87

INDIVIDUAL STUDY QUESTIONS   89

Gangs   90

Drugs   93

Alcohol   95

Family   97

Future   99

7 Steps for Growth, Development and Transition...   100

My Notes: 101

Order Form   102

ACKNOWLEDGMENTS

First and foremost I would like to thank my Lord and Savior, Jesus Christ for blessing me with such a unique vision, for such a monumental collaboration. I could not have persisted through such a tedious assignment, without the strength and guidance from the Holy Spirit. Thank you Father God, I bless you and forever praise you.

To my wife Valarie (Bun); we did it. We are more than conquerors through Christ Jesus. I Love You. Let's continue to run the race set before us. Thank you for all your support throughout this process.

To my Sons Derrick, Relonzo, Jr., and Amillion; you all can achieve anything. Trust in God and believe in yourselves. Learn from my mistakes and never repeat them. Never cave in —never give up! Stand tall and keep it positive. Keep God first in your lives always.

Momma I love you; you always encouraged me to change. You are one of the strongest women I know and I thank God you're my mother. Thank God for giving your son a new plan, a new path and a new life. Better days are ahead Momma.

Dad, thank you for changing your life. I'm glad to have you back in my life in a positive way. A journey of a thousand miles begins with the first step; I'm proud of you. I love you. Stay focused.

To my siblings Moneet, Aisha, Dannell and Quinesha; we've all been through the Storm. Now God has elevated us to higher ground. Let's appreciate it and enjoy it.

Aisha, look to the hills from which cometh your help, your help cometh from the Lord. I love you Sis.

Dannell, I love you Lil' Bro. Seek God; he is always a very present help in the time of trouble. I'm always gonna lift you up on my shoulders.

Grandma, I appreciate all the wisdom you never hesitated to share. You're the best Grandma in the world to me. I love you, and thank you.

Uncle Ron, The Boss of the Fam, thank you for everything. You were always there and you taught me a lot. Aunty Jean, I'll never forget the lessons I've learned from you. Aunty Rena, we grew up like siblings and I'll never forget when you tried to cover for me. Aunty Valencia, you've always been there with us no matter what. I love y'all; keep the faith!

Cousin Rachelle, we went through the stages of life together from day one. I love you. Ronnesha, thank you for all of the insight and knowledge you've shared. I couldn't have established Total Solidarity Publishing without you facilitating the process. I love you.

Ronald Jr., Ryan, Earl, Warren, and James, the love won't stop. You're like my Brothers; this is how we gotta get it now, so let's push and let's do it! To all my cousins, which are too many to name; hold on to God's unchanging hand. Walk by faith not by sight.

To all my nieces and nephews, Uncle Dell loves you all dearly. Don't let anything or anybody hold you down; be strong. There's nothing I wouldn't do for you. I'm in your corner to the fullest. Keep God first, live positive, make wise choice's and fear not because God is with you all.

Uncle Carl and Aunty Lydia, my Pastor and Spiritual Father and my First Lady; thank you for everything, I truly appreciate and love you for being who you are to me. I truly extend my deepest gratitude to you for everything you've been in my life. I love you both.

To Love and Unity Community Church of God in Christ; I'm so elated to be a member of such an anointed ministry. Thank you all for all the love and support. "We are better together." I thank God for the teachings I have received from The C.O.G.I.C., Incorporated, founded by Bishop Charles Harrison Mason.

To the McCorkle family in Chicago, Illinois, I love you all. Renard "Nod" and Ericka Carter, I love you both. Thank you for being there for me, words will never be able to express my gratitude. Nod, you've been an excellent example and I will never forget the things you taught me. Elder Randy Carter, thank you for all your efforts; may God continue to bless you in all of your endeavors. Uncle Shawn, you supported me and opened my eyes to many things about life. Aunty Rita, thanks for all your words of encouragement.

To the DANGERFIELD family, the SHAW family, the RICHARD family, the McCORKLE family, the MELCHOR family, and The JOHNSON family; I love you.

Brother Eriq Hayles and Sister Candy Evess Thomas, thank you for all you've done with this project. God Bless. To anyone I didn't mention please forgive me, but know that we are family and I love you all.

HEAVEN OR HELL

DEDICATION

This book is dedicated in memory of Joe McCorkle Jr., Eddie McCorkle, Sr., Charlie McCorkle, Delvon McCorkle, Benjamin Jones III (B. Jay), Dwayne Young, Jerry Armstrong, Stephon Lucas, Calvin Moore, and Darren Elliot

FOREWARD

This is written for the sole purpose of giving the world a full glimpse of the harsh and brutal realities that many of our youth are confronted with daily. In turn, this book can be used as a meaningful and effective tool to prevent our youth from joining gangs, selling drugs, etc. Furthermore, if anyone has an active involvement in gangs, drugs or any form of negativity, this body of work could be used as a compass, to save someone's life from the ramifications of jails, prisons and ultimately death. This book can also be used to introduce Jesus Christ to all those who are lost in this world. Heaven and Hell are real places. Hopefully, this book will facilitate bringing that fact to the consciousness of the masses.

This particular body of work could not have been accomplished without the inmates opening their hearts and sharing their lives. I would like to personally salute each and every participant of this project. I appreciate your sincere efforts in building this body of work. Thank you, and may God continue to bless you all.

In this body of work, we have a group of seasoned individuals who know from experience what gangs, drugs, and negativity will do to you, as most of them are now serving life sentences. Some have been incarcerated for the last 30 years; the youth of today can learn from their mistakes. None of them ever imagined they would spend the rest of their lives in prison, but it happens every day.

We are all a part of the human race, no matter to what race or religion one may belong. We are all connected! Therefore, it is our civic duty to participate in making our world a more peaceful environment for all humankind. I conclude on this note: "Each one; teach one, to pursue an alternative method contrary to negativity.

Violence is not the answer! If this thought is brought into action, then I truly believe we can live in a more harmonious world.

Psalms 34:1: Depart from evil, and do good, seek peace, and pursue it.

Respectfully,

Relonzo "Dell" Richard, Sr.

Testimonial of Relonzo "Dell" Richard, Sr.

I was born and raised on the notorious East Side of South Central, Los Angeles. Throughout my adolescent years, I lived in several neighborhoods, all of them were gang and crime infested. Modern day wars zones. I grew up in a home where verbal abuse and domestic violence, was a regular occurrence. Any given day, my father would beat my mother in front of my siblings and me. Sometimes I was beaten by my father for diminutive infractions.

My father became profoundly addicted to crack cocaine in the mid 1980's. As a result, our socio-economic status declined rapidly. There were days when food was scarce, there was times when our utilities would get shut off. No matter how tedious life became, my mother lived the life of a devout Christian (we just about lived in church). We would go to church three or four times a week. For me, Church was always an enjoyable and edifying experience. As soon as we returned home from Church, it seemed like we lived in hell. Sometimes I felt like my father was Satan and our home was hell! My mother always made sure all her children prayed together every night.

One New Year's Eve, we were all in my mother's room praying. My father abruptly interrupted showing total contempt for our prayer time. He took me outside in our backyard, put a gun in my hand and told me to shoot it in the air. I was only 9 or 10 years old, so I was having difficulty pulling the trigger. He stood behind me and facilitated my aiming and firing several shots. This left me dazed and confused simultaneously, as well as sparking my interest for guns. My inception to a criminal mentality slowly evolved from that night forward.

I started stealing bikes from local neighborhood kids. The craving for criminality started ascending within me. The corner stores became an everyday target for my shop lifting ventures. I would steal anything I could: chips, sodas, candy bars, etc. I became more sophisticated in my ventures, and elevated myself to stealing from supermarkets. I knew the correct stores to steal from and the precise time; as time progressed, I prided myself for never getting caught. I learned where my father kept a marijuana stash, and then I frequently stole handfuls and sold it to local weed smokers.

As time progressed so did my negative behavior. At school, my grades declined; I fought with other kids and bullied the kids I considered to be weak. I was also witnessing my family infrastructure crumbling, right before my very eyes. My father's crack cocaine addiction had reached an all-time low. He started selling all of our appliances. First, all the televisions disappeared, secondly all the VCR's disappeared, and then our bikes. My clothes vanished, the microwave, the toaster, and then anything else of value suddenly disappeared. Until finally we were left with absolutely nothing, and when I say nothing I mean exactly that.

I was flabbergasted that my father sold everything we had to support his crack habit. I remember feeling utterly dismayed, betrayed and embarrassed. I resented my mother for allowing it to happen. Furthermore, I resented God for subjecting my siblings and me to such brutal treatment, and horrific events. I hated my father for all the pain and suffering he was causing. Ultimately, I took all the pain and disappointment and turned to the streets; I started gang banging. I joined the East Side Q102 Neighborhood East Coast Crips. The homies became my new family; I started slangin crack cocaine when I was 13 years old. At 14 years old, I was convicted and incarcerated for assault and battery and sent to Camp Munz, for 6 months, when I was released, I was on probation. From that point on, I was in and out of Juvenile Hall. At the age of 15, I was sent to Camp Holton, for possession of a firearm and probation violation. Once I was released, I went back to slangin crack again. I was becoming well known for successfully slangin crack. I even started slangin crack to my father on a daily basis. The more money I made, the more recklessly I began to live; I had no regard for anybody.

In 1991 when I was 17, I was arrested for possession of crack and possession of a firearm. I was already on probation, so the Judge sentenced me to the California Youth Authority. There the board sentenced me to 18 months minimum. I was shipped to Preston Youth Correctional Facility in Ione, CA, a well-known Gladiator school. In those days, Preston's reputation was notorious as being a place where only the strong survived and the weak were devoured. I became very insidious and took my Cripin to a new level. I became one of the most prestigious Crips there.

In 1992, I was transferred to Youth Training School (YTS). My violent behavior continued towards all enemies in YTS; the Crips and Bloods were involved in an all-out war. I immediately rendered my full participation. In 1993, the landscape took a sudden change in YTS. While on the recreation yard, 30 Southern Hispanic inmates launched a violent and furiously brutal attack on eight black inmates. I was stabbed in the left arm in that unfortunate event; later on that year, I was granted parole. Back on the streets after a 2-year bid, I picked up where I left off. I went back to banging and slangin crack, with no positive outlook.

I absconded parole, and within 60 days was back incarcerated for a parole violation. I sat in the Los Angeles County jail for four months and then released. Upon my release, my first destination was my neighborhood; to get back to the hood, to hang out with the homeboys and home girls, and slang and bang. The very next day after my release was January 9, 1994; while gambling in the hood I had a premonition and decided to leave. Me and my homeboy were sitting in his car rolling a blunt and talking; two unfamiliar individuals ran up to the driver and passenger windows and opened fire on us. I was shot a total of five times; one bullet hit me directly in the heart. The same GOD I resented for over 15 years, I immediately called upon to save me. I vehemently pleaded, "GOD please don't let me die; I'm too young. I don't wanna die Jesus. Save me," is what I pleaded before losing consciousness. When I woke up I couldn't believe it; I survived, battered bruised and wounded but I survived. I was so thankful; I thanked God for the grace he had bestowed upon me. For the first time in my life, throughout my recuperation I gave serious contemplation about my life.

Nevertheless, once I was released from the hospital, I was back banging in the hood. My gratitude toward God quickly evaporated. My primary concern became the Q102, East Coast Crips. I eventually violated parole again and in 1995, I was sent back to YTS for four months. Then while I was incarcerated, I started to think about giving up on the Crip life. I wanted to hang up my blue flag. The Crip life was a tedious lifestyle, full of pitfalls, and that was something I couldn't ignore.

Once again, I was released. I went back in the hood banging and slangin crack. I began to put more emphasis on hustling. I backed away from the gang banging; I moved up in the dope game and started accumulating large sums of money. I enjoyed my new level of success; I brought new cars, clothes and gaudy jewelry. I flaunted my money; I had my choice of beautiful women. The more money I made, the more I began to spend. I lived like this for years, Ballin'... the life was good and I was enjoying it. There is an old saying, "easy come easy go." What comes up must come down. With a series of mismanagement and bad business deals along with excessive gambling, the party was over. I went broke, I came back up, and I went broke again. This process became the norm; one minute I was up the next minute I was down.

Tired of the inconsistency, I made a rash decision and committed an armed robbery. I was captured on camera. In September of 2000, I was incarcerated and eventually sentenced to 12 years in state prison, and ordered to serve 85% of the 12-year sentence. After being sentenced, my outlook was gloomy and dark. I was angry and I felt totally hopeless. Once I arrived at prison, I became more negative. I poured all my energy into cripin. I spent an excessive amount of time reading and studying. I had a tremendous desire to elevate myself in the ranks of the Crips while in prison. For that reason, I utilized my time wisely and took advantage of the knowledge I learned. As the years began to pass, I began to ascend in the ranks on the prison yard. I mastered all aspects of prison life within three years. I lead large groups of Crips in exercise routines, such as burpies and various calisthenics. I was successful in all of our various economic endeavors. I became insidious in the arenas of political and military science.

After seven years into my incarceration, it became tremendously tedious. The life was weighing on me heavily. I noticed after decades of living the crip life I didn't have anything to show for it but war wounds and tattoos. I came to the realization that the crip life brought my family and me more pain and suffering than anything else did. I began to get more displeased with that entire way of life. I wanted more for my family and myself; I began to crave something of more substance. I decreased my involvement with my constituents. I started to seek something else. One night someone invited me to a

Bible study. I was reluctant to attend initially because I was high and strapped with a knife; but, I still attended. I enjoyed what I heard.

The next day, I decided to go and listen to the Bible study again. I felt at ease after attending. I was struggling inside; I wanted to change my life but I didn't know how I could while I was still in prison. I was concerned with what the homies would think of me; I didn't want to appear as if I had turned weak and soft. So, even though I had started attending Bible studies, I was still smoking weed and drinking pruno and I continued to carry a knife wherever I went. After a while, I noticed as time went on, that the weed wasn't getting me high anymore. Instead of being high, I would get a headache; my desire to drink pruno dissolved. I just didn't like the way it made me feel.

On June 7, 2007, I got into a fight on the yard; as a result, I was sent to the hole (AD-SEG). While in AD-SEG, I was released to attend crip yard. The Lil' homies asked me to lead the exercise regimen; I declined the offer. I didn't want to be on the crip yard. Every day I began contemplating my existence. I wanted more out of life than prison. I felt profoundly remorseful for all the pain I caused my family, especially my mother. I thought about all the horrible things I had done throughout my life. I thought about all of my homeboys I had lost to this life style; for the first time, I asked myself if all this pain and misery were worth it. I immediately concluded: no, it is not worth it. I sat there and wept uncontrollably. I ended up on my knees crying out to God Jesus Christ. I asked God to forgive me of my sins, all of them. I asked God to help me and to come into my life and create a new heart within me. I realized how selfish and self-centered I had been.

From that day on, my mind was made up; I wouldn't travel the road of destruction any longer. I started reading the Bible, and I dedicated hours to reading and studying the Bible every day. I felt so much better; I felt as if a heavy load had been lifted off me. I felt so peaceful. Every day I dedicated time for fervent prayer. I promised God after I was released back to the main line I would continue to seek him. I was transferred to California State Prison, Los Angeles County. I told the homies that I was on my spiritual quest. I went to Bible studies faithfully; I stopped smoking weed, and I stopped drinking pruno. I didn't carry a weapon either. One by one, I overcame all of my vices. The homies were completely shocked at my transformation. I eventually started my own Bible study in the cellblock. I took time and passed out tracks and I helped others become sturdy in their transformation. Even though I'm still in prison, I'm FREE. I'm no longer enslaved to that old way of thinking. I have a new mentality now, I'm not perfect, I'm not where I should be, but I'm not what I was; I'm a work in progress.

I want to inform the Youth: learn from me and from my mistakes. Save yourself and loved ones from this sort of pain. The road of negativity is a dead end road. If you're gang banging and selling drugs, get out while you have a chance. Love yourself and your FAMILY enough to live in the positive realm. Explore your options in the positive realm. If you don't have a personal relationship with GOD, accept him into your life. I encourage you to read John 10:10 and Philippians 4:13.

Respectfully your Brother in Christ

Relonzo "Dell" Richard, Sr.

Look out for my book HEAVEN OR HELL, Vol. 2

and other books from Total Solidarity Publishing

Testimonial of Rico

This is how God changed my life from an Evil lost sinner in to a Saint.

First and foremost, I want to give God the Father and Jesus Christ, our personal Lord and Savior, all the honor praise and glory for saving me and braking the shackles of condemnation from my hands and feet. Thank you, Jesus. In Christ, I live, move and truly have my being... My Brother's and Sister's, I have a lot to be thankful for in spite of being incarcerated. God didn't allow the devil to kill me while I was living in my filth and doing everything contrary unto his will and purpose for my life.

My Brothers and Sisters let me share my testimony with you about where God brought me from.

I grew up in Los Angeles with eight others siblings. Unfortunately, I lost both of my parents in 1969. I was raised by my Aunt through marriage who was extremely strict and abusive. I was unable to go outside until Friday. My siblings and I had to stay in the house and study ten words out of the encyclopedia, and if you missed just one of those words, you were going to get beat with an extension cord. This left me very angry and wanting to kill the world and anyone that would try to hurt me or my siblings, especially my little sister. I felt so unloved by my Aunt at home; I decided to turn to the streets, when I was able to get out of the house. Which lead me to gang activity, after looking up to my cousin who was a very active gang member from 5-Tray Avalon. His name was Big Brownie; he was a very notorious person in his day.

When I was 13 years old, I wanted to be just like my cousin, notorious with a reputation that made people afraid of me. I always felt that you needed a reputation to make it far in life. Little did I know there were consequences of having a notorious reputation, like death or doing a lengthy prison sentence.

At the age of 13 years old, I tried to start my very own crip set, East Side 83rd Street Block Crip. Unfortunately, it didn't take off, as I wanted it to. The majority of the kids in my old neighborhood were good kids and didn't want to get caught up in gang activity, so I decided to leave it alone. Until I met up with an old girlfriend, who I later married and had kids with at the age of 17. Yvette stayed on the East Side of Los Angeles between Main, Broadway and 61st. I started hanging out in her neighborhood and met Lil' Sad and some more of the fellas from 6-Duce Neighborhood East Coast Crip. As I begin to hang out with them, I found myself going out shooting at rival gang members, a blood set called Swans. At the age of 18 years old, my little sister was going out with one of them, who I later shot for putting his hands on her.

Right after shooting Wayne, I began terrorizing my community and neighborhood through gang violence and selling drugs, which landed me in the county jail for a year back in 1978. Big mistake, because I was in and out of jail every year from 1978 to 1984. March of 85, I went to Chino State Prison for attempted murder on my ex-wife, Yvette for cheating on me with a member of a blood gang called 62 Brims. I did 2 years of a 4-year sentence. I was released from prison in 1987 and I went back to my ex-wife, Yvette.

In April of 1987, I hooked up with my nephew who was a big drug dealer from 67th B.T.H. (Big Time Hustlers). I started selling drugs for him until I was able to sell for myself. Unfortunately, I found myself back in prison in 1987. I stayed out for seven months before I caught a drug case; I did a year violation and got out in 1988. I went back to prison in 1988 for having a gun in my Cadillac. I received 16 months for the gun. My year violation ate up the 16 months because I was only going to do 8 months off the 16 months.

I got out in 1989 and my parole officer told me that if I go back to jail or prison, the courts were going to hit me with the habitual criminal act, which means I would receive life in prison for being a known criminal. Unfortunately, the courts felt like if I got into any more trouble, I just didn't know how to do right or live a productive life amongst society.

Well, I stayed out of prison for 2 ½ years and my kids and family were so proud of me.

I met my second wife, Jeanette in 1990. We had a son in 1992. I took Jeanette out of an abusive relationship. Her oldest son Anthony's father didn't like the fact that Jeanette was with me now. He and I begin shooting at each other, which brought the evilness out of me again. For 2½ years, I tried to live a productive life without getting into trouble. Unfortunately, Anthony Sr. brought the monster back out of me and before I knew it, I shot seven people and killed one, which landed me back in jail, fighting murder and attempted murder charges.

I fought the death penalty for 15 months. Then I decided to end my life by hanging myself with a sheet after the death of my oldest son Calvin, who decided to commit suicide by shooting himself in the head at the age of 14. Jeanette went back to Anthony Sr. I felt I had nothing else to live for so I decided to kill myself. I hung so long I had defecated on myself. The police in the Los Angeles county jail pronounced me dead, and rushed me to L.C.M.C. Hospital and revived me.

"I give Jesus the Glory"

To shorten the rest of my testimony I decide to give my life to Jesus, because after receiving life in prison I was still miserable and needed peace in my life. A brother in Christ told me Jesus could give me that peace. I decided to give Jesus a try. I felt like I had nothing to lose and a lot to gain. I tried Jesus and have been saved now for 11 ½ years. I gave my life unto the Lord, September 25 1997. Jesus is who he says he is. My Brothers and Sisters, if you don't know Jesus as your Lord and Savior, you have nothing to lose, but a whole lost to gain. By the way, my cousin Big Brownie is a preacher in Texas.

"Ain't God Good?"

Psalms 23:6: Surely goodness and mercy shall follow me all the days of my life: and I will dwell in the house of the Lord forever.

Peace and God Speed!!

I love you in the Lord, your brother in Christ,

Rico

Testimonial of Dennis Parmenter

My name is Dennis; I am doing life in prison for the murder of my estranged wife, "Estella"

There was a time in my life when I thought that I had everything I needed in my life, but I was still unhappy. I did everything I could to gratify myself; doing drugs, I even had an affair with another woman. I knew almost nothing about God or what Christ did for me.

Slowly but surely I lost everything: my mind, my job, my wife and finally all my friends. I even gained 90 pounds. Eventually I even became so lost in sin that I murdered my wife.

When I woke up in jail, I could not believe what I had done. I was filled with shame and remorse, and I had hurt so many.

Sitting all alone in that jail cell there was a Bible; and for the first time in my life, I read the word of God. It was in that cell that I asked Jesus for forgiveness for my sins and accepted him for my Lord and Savior.

As the years have passed, I have continued to learn the word of God and apply it to my life. I've been so blessed. Sometimes people who are here ask me, "Why are you so happy" and I tell them it is because I know that I am saved.

One time recently, an officer here asked me how much time I was doing. I told him Life-Without Parole. He said "No!"

I replied, I have more than that, I have victory over this world through Jesus Christ."

Dennis Parmenter

P-15178

Testimony of Gerald Benoit

At an early age, I was introduced to the Lord Jesus Christ, by my grandmother. She had me and my brother Seanon at Church every Sunday; for Sunday school, morning service, and then afternoon service. To hear some Gospel groups perform, we even went back for Sunday night service. But hearing those gospel groups was what I liked. My grandmother put me to work in our church; by the way, our church's name is Pleasant Hill Missionary Baptist Church. I was in the youth-adult choir, and on the Jr. Usher Board. I had to help sell dinners every other Saturday; anywhere I was needed I helped. As I stated before, I was into gospel groups. I became a part of the Morris Brothers Plus One, a gospel group, at around 10 or 11 years old; my love was singing. Somehow, the group broke up and then we all started doing our own thing. Some did R&B and others, other things.

I think at around 13 I got introduced to weed and girls and started doing worldly stuff. Around this time, I found out I had a wicked tongue and got into the pimp world; I did that for a while. At about 16 years old, I gave that life up and went back to my first love, singing gospel. I got into another group, the W.D. Brothers. I gave the pimp lifestyle up but not the weed, and found myself back out in the world. Now I am doing more than weed, I am into cocaine.

At age 19, I started going to jail, in and out doing the same thing. At 23, I found myself going to prison. I was sent to Vacaville State Prison. While in prison, I met Rev. Roy Davis. He was a prisoner and a Pastor. Rev. Davis became my mentor and I learned a lot from him, but I didn't want to let go and let God.

I ended up in the Shu (Security Housing Unit) in Pelican Bay State prison. I did 5 years and 7 days. I was released August 19, 1996, and the first day I got out of prison I started back with cocaine. Seven months later, I was right back in the Sacramento County Jail. In August 1998, I was sentenced to 56 years to life. While doing my time in Sacramento County Jail, I attended Bible study; the teacher was a neighbor of my father's. Well his class got me back on track with the Lord. I was doing well until I got back behind the prison walls. I was placed in Folsom State Prison in November 1998. While there, I did the Homie thing. I left there in 1999, and I was sent to Calipatria State Prison. While there, I went to the hole. I stayed in trouble up until the year 2000.

I was sent to Salinas Valley State Prison and really stepped away from the Lord. I sold dope and wine and hung with the Homies. I did everything that wasn't of God. April 2002 they locked me up in a cell (they called it Confined Too Quarters (CTQ)) for over a month for an investigation. During this time, I got close to Lord again. During this confinement, there was nothing in the cell with me but a Bible and radio. So I had many up close talks with the Lord. I made a promise to my grandmother and aunt that every time the doors to the chapel opened I will be there. I know I made commitments to them, but it was really to God. I gave my life back to the Lord and I have been with him since. I'm not going to say that I haven't sinned, the Bible tells us that we all sin, read 1 John 1:8. What I am saying is that I have truly found the Lord with all of my heart, soul, and mind. I can't, and won't, and will never turn back around.

Thank you, Father God for giving your Son's life for me, thank you Jesus for saving me and thank you Holy Spirit for comforting me.

I Love You, Thank you, Thank you, Thank you, Amen

Thank you for allowing me to share my testimony with you may God Bless you and keep you.

Respectfully,

Gerald Benoit

H25851

Testimonial of DeAndre Griffen

I grew up in a Christian family, so I've always been familiar with Jesus, but I never really took Christ seriously. When I went to church, it was never really to glorify the Lord it was to glorify myself. It was a big thing back when I was young, to tell your family, neighbors and friends that you went to church; I didn't even know the significance of why I really went. I didn't even understand what the Preacher was talking about; all I knew was that it was something about some God or Jesus; that was what my family would say.

I was six years old when I moved out of the Nickerson Gardens projects. My whole family was from over there. Everybody in my family that grew up over there never was successful; they all gang banged, sold drugs or did robberies. My mother was trying to find a better life for me and for my twin brother (who I'm older than by 1 minute). We moved into another neighborhood and everything seemed cool. It felt good to be out the projects and into a completely new setting. The street was super cool, no gang bangers or nonsense was in the atmosphere, but that would all change soon. Now I see why they say, "You have to accept the good with the bad."

The years had passed and my twin brother and I were getting older. My mother had stopped working when she was pregnant with my little brother. My twin and I are 10 years older than our little brother. We were 12 and our little brother was two when all Hell broke loose. Times had become even rougher for my twin and me. It was already bad enough; Mother had to take care of two of us as it was, so for a newborn coming into the world, it made it even more difficult. Me and my twin had stopped getting all the new Jordans and latest outfits; we stopped wearing our gear (clothes) one time and started wearing them until we couldn't wear them anymore. We started getting hand me downs from our older homies.

Times had really gotten rough. It was at this specific time when we got recruited into the Crip life; we started gang banging and claiming West Side Raymond Avenue Crips. We were going to Henry Clay Middle School. I never went to school to learn nothing. All I went for was to show off, and to be mister almighty, acting like I'm all tough. My brother and I had started going to school and selling drugs for our older homies. Every day after school they would come pick us up with the other homies. We would go around the school ground asking who had a problem with our set, knowing nobody would say anything. I must admit, having that type of power felt good, it made me feel like a giant. My twin and I were headed for the road of destruction and we just couldn't see it.

Time passed and we started going to Locke High School; by this time, we had started packing pistols. I had a 32 revolver and my brother had a 22. When all our other gang banging homies found out we were packing pistols they started giving us respect. Especially the way my brother was showing off, walking around with his pistol out shouting out the hood. I mean just going full-fledged. It was at that time we would soon find out nothing bad lasts too long.

While we were walking to school one day packing the 22 revolver, two L.A.P.D. Officers pulled up on us, searched us and found the gun in my brother's backpack. My brother was hauled to Juvenile Hall and was later released because it was his first arrest. That wasn't the last time for him or me.

I started burglarizing houses, and stealing cars; that led to much bigger crimes. Every time I got caught for a crime, Juvenile Hall would let me go. When I got caught for a house burglary I had to spend three months in Camp Resneck at Challenger; but that still didn't stop me. I just didn't learn my lesson; I didn't see the crash coming. I just kept on like a big crash dummy. It wasn't until I was 16 that my eyes would start to be opened. I was trying to play follow the leader and be like my homeboys, because they were putting in work and having all the flashy things. I wanted to copy them and do the same; yea I paid the price. I got caught on sight committing attempted murder with a firearm. At first, I thought the victim was dead, I shot him dead in the head and he was completely laid out. When I was at the police station, the officers were teasing me telling me I would get life in prison. So I was all messed up. I thought my life had gone down the drain. I later found out through my rival enemies that I didn't actually kill the dude. That's when I really thanked God, for the first time in my life. While I was in juvenile hall fighting my case I started to pray and read my Bible, but I was still fully gang banging. I would always ask God if he would just give me another chance, I would promise to be good. God knew I was lying, and I most definitely knew I was lying. That's why God didn't let me out.

As I was in juvenile hall fighting my case I was tried as an adult; they didn't have any sympathy for me. I started going to adult court with all the dudes from the LA County Jail. Time was passing and finally I turned 18 years old. Sylmar juvenile hall couldn't wait to send me off to the LA County Jail. I was a little frightened; I had been hearing all these different war stories about the county jail, how dudes were getting brutally beat up, stomped out, tied up to bunks and gang raped by their rivals. I wasn't for sure if all these rumors were true but it sure did have me on my toes; I was on red alert the moment I stepped in to the place.

When I hit the 4300 floor, it was on and popping; two bloods banged on me and I banged back. When they found out who I was, they went and told their Blood partners who were also my rival enemies. My enemy came and banged on me and I banged right back, I told him he could catch a fade (fight) if he wanted to. So we set the fight up. I wasn't satisfied so the next morning I went down to the Blood floor and told him I needed that fade again, so we fought again and I felt more relieved.

I witnessed some crazy stuff in the LA County Jail. I remember when I was sneaking over to the 2300 floor, I saw this one dude tied up underneath the bunk. Yea the LA County Jail is no place to fool around with; you have to be extremely careful, especially as a gang member.

Time was passing on and I was going back and forth to court; things weren't looking too well. This is when I first started to feel the pain they were talking about (life) and all types of nonsense. I couldn't see myself doing life in prison. For me just to say, that I accepted that as a deal just didn't set right with me. I literally begged the Judge for any date, so he gave me 25 years flat, with 5 years' time served. For the first time, I really saw my Mom shed tears for me. I was crushed. I tried not to show any kind of weakness, I told my Mom it would be all right.

My journey started from there on. I went back to the LA County Jail for a very short period of time, and was later shipped off to my first prison to start my time. When I first got to prison, I was blind to a whole a lot of stuff, so I didn't trust nothing or nobody. I ran into my homie from my neighborhood and right off the top, he moved me to the same building the homies were in. My homie had been in prison for 10 plus years so he knew how everything ran. He stayed on my head about learning my surroundings. By me being new to prison life and on a level 4 yard, he had to make sure I was on point. Anything can happen within a snap of a finger so it was important to stay ready. As time passed on, I got the feeling of how the program was run. I got me a knife made, that I usually kept on me. Sooner or later, I knew something was going to happen where I was going to have to use it.

At that specific time in life, I was banged out, so I was eager to use the weapon and prove myself. A time came where we had to discipline one of our own kind for violating some serious rules; so we had to do a mission and the mission was done. That was my first time getting pepper sprayed and man; the pepper spray ain't no joke. That stuff really had me on fire. I got sprayed all over; I was drenched wet. It seemed as though someone took some gasoline, poured it all over me, stuck a match and lit me on fire. That stuff was in my eyes, burning my ear lobes and upper back. My nut sack felt like a volcano exploded. Even though we took showers, when we got out the showers we still could smell the pepper spray coming from out of our pores.

Me and my crimey were sent to the hole pending the hearing on our new case for carrying out the discipline handed down by the older homies. I must admit that being in the hole was very stressful; no television, no radio and no CD player and you can only have a limited amount of your property. You can't use the phone to call your family or loved ones or none of that good stuff. Being in the hole is a prison inside a prison. All your rights and freedom are taken away. This is basically designed to break you as a hard core individual. After so long of being in there, you get to telling yourself, like damn, I ain't coming back to this place, getting handcuffed every day, everywhere you go, limited showers, limited yard. You have to be stuck in a little box cage, with another man all day; I mean it's just not cool. I can't speak for the next man, but because I hadn't been in prison three months before I did my first mission, being in the hole really got to me. Not being able to talk to my mother or get packages when my love ones wanted to send them to me, it was really getting to me. I started to think and tell myself, this wasn't the way I want to do my time. I no longer wanted to be a part of gangs. I was through being a gang member. I started to search for God. I really didn't know where to start but I knew I wanted to better myself. Time passed on and I beat my case. It was dropped down to a battery on an inmate with a deadly weapon.

I was transferred to High Desert State Prison, which is way up in Northern California in Susanville. Being in High Desert was my first time seeing snow and making snowballs. As a little kid, that was always a dream I had wished for. Well some dreams come true. Being in High Desert was difficult for a youngster such as me; they were really gang banging at that prison. Most of the time we stayed on lock down, because of somebody getting stabbed or beaten. There was a whole bunch of discipline going on. I stayed out the way and away from that nonsense. My whole goal was growing and perfecting myself. I wanted better for myself but because I was at a prison that always stayed on lock down, and only had limited resources, it was hard for me. It was crazy because I was only 19 and most youngsters my age were still primetime gang banging.

I wasn't into the gang activity anymore; I must admit that I felt like an outsider for the first time in my life. My young Crip homeboys would always try to convince me that I could come back home, which means start back Criping. Sometimes it was tempting but the one thing that always stopped me from rejoining was taking part in gang politics. It's bad enough that I lost my freedom trying to put in work for a hood that really didn't give a crap about me. So to continue to do the same thing while already in prison just seemed really foolish; it's really like saying you don't care too much about your family or loved ones because you still choose to be a part of something that doesn't care about you. I've seen too many dudes who were either trying to stay out of trouble because they were going home soon or because they were going to a lower level prison. But because they were a part of gang politics, they were obligated to participate whenever their group moved or got into any confrontation. It was either participate or take a discipline for not participating. Trust me, I think you'll be better off in a fight against another group; at least you know who and what you're up against. When you're getting a discipline, you never know who or what is coming. It could be your closest homie that is sent to be the one to set you up and stab you in your back. That's why I made a decision that would benefit me and keep me out of harm's way. Though I made a positive decision, the decision wasn't easy.

As the time passed and I was finding myself searching for "God" the harder it got for me. It's very hard to do right when 95% of your environment is negative. While I was at High Desert State Prison searching for a personal relationship with "God," I ran across a good brother who really took a liking to me. This dude was real good with legal work. He told me that I had a good heart and didn't belong at that prison. He put the proper paperwork in so that I could get the help I needed to grow. I then became a DD2 inmate, which means I was diagnosed with a speech impediment, and a learning disability. I was then transferred to Lancaster State Prison where my life would soon take on a new path.

When I first stepped on the grounds on the A-yard facility at Lancaster State Prison, I knew things would be difficult because I wasn't banging anymore. To establish myself as a non-affiliate was hard to do, when I first pulled up, because you have dudes who knew me from my past at other prisons and they told dudes from my old neighborhood that I just pulled up. So, I had all these dudes coming up to me banging on me, asking where I was from and other questions. I would always tell them that I had given my life to "God" and I'm through with that life. I could tell some dudes weren't tripping but some were. At this specific time, I believed in God but I was still in the flesh, and I had a hand into the worldly life. I learned later that you just can't do both. As the Bible says in James 1:8: ". . . a double minded man is unstable in all his ways." And I know for sure I was unstable in my ways; I was one foot in and one foot out. I started facing some harsh trials and tribulations. It seemed as though everybody was against me; though there were some dudes encouraging me to continue to do right the majority was just negative. Most of the time I just worked out and kicked it by myself; dudes from my own neighborhood talked to me but I sensed hatred in the air. Certain dudes who knew me before weren't even talking to me. I really felt like an outsider.

Later on, I was faced with a situation where I was being belittled and being taken advantage of; I was already in a low state of mind as I was going through family problems. I was around someone extremely miserable who wanted me to be the same way. Because this person knew that I was feeling down and vulnerable, this person would try to manipulate and take advantage of me. Having pressure on you can sometimes be worse than death. It can mentally mess you up if you're not strong enough. I was going through it all and didn't have anyone to talk to. I started having suicidal thoughts; I thought the world was over for me. I just didn't want to live knowing I would have to abide in a harsh environment. Thoughts ran through my head telling me "I refuse to deal with these obstacles." It wasn't until a good Christian Brother; Brother Keith came into my life that I was revived. It was a summer day in July; I was out on the yard lost in my own world, stressed out on the edge, and not knowing what I was going to do next. If it wasn't for Brother Keith coming and witnessing the word of God to me, God knows what I would of done next. Brother Keith and I prayed that day. We talked about the Lord Jesus Christ. When Brother Keith first walked up to me as a Stranger during that time, I thought he was just another faker preaching the word. But I later found out that Brother Keith is one of the most sincere, caring, loving and dedicated dudes of Christ Jesus.

I still remember the first words that came from out of his mouth. He said, "Do you know Jesus loves you?"

I said "Naw, not really." Brother Keith then gave me a very short sermon and for the first time in a long time, I felt good. I needed that comfort, care and love. Before he departed, he did a prayer with me that I used to prevail and overcome the stress, obstacles and all the problems that I was facing. Soon, like three days later, I was able to get out and away from that miserable person who was causing me much stress and turmoil. I know that God had answered my prayers. Two weeks later, I accepted Christ Jesus as my Lord and Savior. My life has been anointed and blessed ever since. Though I'm faced with trials and tribulations, I know as the Bible says in Roman 8:37, "we are more than conquerors through Christ Jesus."

Yours Truly,

DeAndre Griffen

F33004

Testimonial of Charlie K. Jones

As a boy growing up in the streets of Compton (Original Front Hood Compton Crip), coupled with a false sense of what life was all about, I began to get active with the homies. I eventually dropped out of school and started robbing and selling drugs. Ultimately, this progressed into attempted murders, and unfortunately, murder.

When I got arrested for murder back in March 1990; I was only 18 years old. The judge at that time sentenced me to 30 years to life and told me "he wished he could be handing me a diploma or a certificate instead of a sentence." Although the judge was reluctant to give me a life sentence, he made it clear to me that 30 years to life was the only sentence I could receive for that crime and that he had to follow the law.

After all this, you would think I had enough and learned my lesson. But I didn't, I actually got worse! Because now my thoughts was that since I had life, I wasn't ever gonna get out anyway. All those years I relied on drugs and alcohol, which I thought then would eliminate those unresolved feelings of anxiety and depression. One day I was sitting on my bunk in the cell when all of a sudden these really nice people came to my cell door. They asked me was I saved, and I told them that I received Christ into my life when I was younger, but that I didn't know if I fully understood at that age. Then he said to me that God loves me and that he died on the cross of Calvary just so I can have eternal life (John 3:16.) As we went over some scriptures in the Bible, which all pointed to God's love for me and others, I made a decision to start living for him. It was then that I began to experience the joy that only comes with walking with God.

"For his anger endures but a moment; in his favor is life: weeping may endure for a night, but joy cometh in the morning" Psalms 30:5

Charlie K. Jones

J-75586

Testimonial of Greg Thomas (aka) Anthony Pitts

First of all, my true name is Gregory Thomas; but I am currently in prison under the alias Anthony Pitts, and I am 46 years old. My personal testimony is quite long.

The summer of 1992, I was serving a 1-year sentence for parole violation. At that time, the only reverence toward God or Jesus Christ was what my parents had instilled in me as a young man living in Los Angeles, and during the summer of 1992 in Folsom Prison.

I was an active 107 Hoover Gang member who wanted nothing to do with God, or the Bible for that matter. Although I would often make an attempt to read the Bible, for some reason there was always some Christian trying to invite me to become a Christian, and because I knew about Jesus Christ, I believed I was already a Christian to some extent.

On November 18, 1992, I was released from prison and excited to be coming home to what I thought was my then girlfriend and our 2-year-old son. As I approached the front door, I could see my girlfriend through the front window of her house laughing and hugging another man. I knocked on the door in a rage saying, "it's me"; but to my surprise, my girlfriend's mother answered the door. She told me that my son was not there, and her daughter, my so-called girlfriend, did not want to see me. She said if I would come back tomorrow, I could see my son, which really made me even angrier. So I demanded my so-called girlfriend, whose name was April come talk to me personally before I would leave, or there would be a problem. Then suddenly April stepped out to the side of her mother at the door to say, "Greg, your son is not here but come back tomorrow."

The guy who I saw her hugging and laughing with in the window yelled, "April is my girl now and you better leave before I shoot you." At that point, the door closed in my face. I went into a rage challenging the other guy.

Soon the Sheriff's department showed up and detained me while they went to the door to verify my story that I was here just out of prison and I was there to see my girlfriend and my son who just turned two years old on November 16, 1992. Once the Sheriffs deputies came back from the house, they said to my surprise that April said we were no longer together and the guy with her was her new boyfriend, and I needed to leave before there's a problem. If I wanted to see my son, he would be at her mother's house tomorrow. I told the officers there must be a mistake, but they insisted that I leave or go to jail for trespassing on private property. With that, I was forced to walk my way back to the nearest bus stop and make my way home to my Mom and family in Long Beach.

At the time I was very bitter and in my mind I vowed to come back soon for revenge. As I got on the bus to Long Beach, all I could do was try to gather my thoughts and emotions over what had just occurred. Instead of going straight to Long Beach, I decided to make a stop in an area between Palmdale and Long Beach where I knew people. With what little money I had left, I decided to get some beer to drink, in an attempt to ease my painful emotions. The beer lead to marijuana, which lead to some cocaine, which soon left me broke disgusted and unable to reach my destination, which was the Long Beach Parole Office within 24 hours and my family.

Thanksgiving was slowly approaching, but by this time, I couldn't even care what could happen. While sitting near a store in an area where lots of drugs are sold and wondering how I would get my next dollar and a possible bus ticket home, I saw a Mexican guy looking to buy drugs so I assured him, I knew where to go. As he followed me to a dark alley, I grabbed him in a headlock and took the $80.00 dollars he had to buy drugs and pushed him down. His last words to me in a deep Spanish accent were "me remember you." Later I would learn that this was a promise and not a statement. I went and found a few friends to get high with on crack cocaine with my money from this robbery, asking myself in my mind, *what am I doing with my life?*

Fresh out of prison and still wearing the same clothes I was paroled from prison in two days earlier, I decided to find somewhere to finish getting high and think deeply about what I was doing here in the Projects alone, instead of going home to my family, after that hurtful ordeal in Palmdale with my son's mother.

After smoking another hit of crack, I looked up and to my surprise I was being approached by to my estimate about 8 to 10 Mexican guys, including the one Mexican that I had robbed earlier, who was speaking directly to me saying the last words he said when I robbed him for his money. They all had sticks and bottles in hand and I slowly stood up in a defensive posture when they all rushed me at once. My last memory of this was feeling something hit me on the back of my head. This was late night November 20, 1992 or early morning November 21, 1992. When I finally awoke at approximately 4:00 am, December 5, 1992, I soon learned that I was on a hospital gurney wrapped in a hospital gown with a tag on my right big toe that read pronounced deceased at 3:24 a.m. I was being wheeled into the hospital morgue at Sierra Memorial Hospital. I sat up on the gurney; several nurses began to scream yell run in panic, while several other doctors and nurses were yelling to me not to move. I didn't know at the time that severe, blunt head trauma is the medical term used to describe a person who has lapsed into a coma. This disables someone from the ability to walk or talk; to make a long story short; I was beaten and left for dead.

When the ambulance picked me up, I had on only my socks, boxers and t-shirt. I had a fresh haircut and trimmed fingernails but no I.D., so I didn't appear to be a homeless transient; but I was listed as John Doe, who was unresponsive with a slight pulse. Between November 21, 1992 and December 5, 1992, doctors tried to revive me but finally gave up and took me off life support. They pronounced me dead at 3:24 a.m. on December 5, 1992. Obviously, God had other plans for me because eventually, I was able to write down my family's phone number. By 6:31a.m., on December 5, 1992 I woke again, after the medical staff decided that my name was Gregory Thomas. As surprised as I was, I was wondering where I was, why was everyone here, and what was going on? In my mind, these were the questions I was asking my numerous family members. Many began to cry because this is not what they were hearing me say. What I soon learned was that for the past two weeks I had been in a coma and eventually pronounced dead only to mysteriously awaken. I could no longer talk or walk as a result of being under the influence of drugs and alcohol and suffering severe blunt head trauma, after being beaten practically to death by a large number of men and left for dead. This is what the paramedics and doctors explained to my Mom. They also told my Mom that I would need extensive pathology and extensive physical therapy in order to at least regain a minimal degree of talking and walking skills over a long period of time.

When my mother explained this to me in that hospital that morning, I was crushed to tears. Then what she told me was that they asked her to leave me in the hospital so that I could get this treatment. To my surprise, my Mom told me that she told the doctors that no matter what they said, she was taking me home today because God is not done with her son yet. Those words never meant then what they mean to me now because at that time I had not accepted Jesus Christ as my Lord and Savior. (Roman 10:9) The fact that I have never ever had one minute of speech pathology or physical therapy to this day should speak for itself about the awesome power of God. I can talk, walk, jump and run as good and as fast as I ever could before suffering these injuries. By 1995 in the county jail on my way back to prison for yet another term, I finally accepted Jesus Christ as my Lord and Savior. If there is one thing I learned in all of this, Jesus Christ is real and Jesus Christ does heal people like me, a former gang member and drug user and abuser.

Psalms 46:1: God is our refuge and strength a very present help in trouble.

"Greg"

Testimonial of Anthony L. Webb

I was raised by a 17-year-old mother and 18-year-old father who didn't know his father, so it was difficult for him to know how to raise a child. It was a decent childhood as I grew up, even though I was brought up in a housing project. I slowly drifted into wrong at about 13 years of age, starting with a little vandalism and a little stolen property, which led to a little drinking and eventually at 16 to a little marijuana smoking, and drug selling.

I wish I had been able to see the snowball effect, because I would have most likely chosen a different path. I dropped out of the 11th grade, moved to Oakland to sell drugs out of a crack house and almost ended up losing my life at a motel. An inner voice, a voice we call a conscience, spoke to me and told me to slow down; but the homeboys, street life and its allure silenced the voice of common sense.

Forward to 1993, I was at a house party in my neighborhood when I got into an argument with a rival gang member and ended up being shot. There was that voice again and again I ignored it. Even when coupled with the pleading of my mother, that was the event that really caused my life to spiral downwards, because now I had to carry a gun.

Flash forward to 1995, I had to *use* a gun. A hard lesson to learn is that when you carry a gun, you will eventually use it. Long story short...My closest dog cooperated with the police and turned me in to get a lighter deal on something he was charged with.

That was 1998. Forward to 2009, I'm in prison with three life sentences without parole, but people tell me that they can't tell that I have that much time. It's because I know what I'm on this planet to do; that is share Jesus Christ and his love. The very thing I was looking for in the streets is the very thing my Grandma was trying to instill in me as a youngster. My greatest desire is for whoever is reading this to take a time-out and listen... to that voice of conscience, that voice of Grandma, that voice of LOVE.

Anthony Webb

P53460

Testimonial of Travielle James Craig

As a child, I had a drug problem. My mother "drug" me to church, every time the doors were open. But over time, my mother stopped going to church; as a result her son became Possie, from a Blood gang called Swans in South Central Los Angeles. In being involved in gangs, I did almost any and every wicked thing under the sun. I sold and used drugs, I shot, robbed, and beat up on people just for the fun of it, or even if they looked at me funny or wore the wrong color, or lived on the wrong side of the street.

I served with all my heart a foreign god. We had a saying called the "SWAN god" and with everything that went on in my life, the "S-god" got the glory. If something good happened, the "S-god" smiled on me; if it was bad, he frowned upon me. I was in bad shape spiritually. I didn't believe in, didn't want to hear about God. I didn't care if I lived or died. I couldn't use religion as a child and it did nothing for me, as I got older. I made up my own will with the "S-god." People would try to tell me about Jesus; I wasn't trying to hear it. I told them to miss me or get beat up. I remember I was in my cell and I didn't want to read a Bible and I thought to myself, nobody else was gonna read it either, so for fun I set it on fire. I continued in this man made religion up until I was arrested at the age of 18 years old.

What started out as two counts of attempted murder eight months later turned into 1st degree murder, which later turned into life without the possibility of parole; all by the age of 19. Here I was sitting in my cell, praying, asking for help but religion couldn't help me. I would later learn that a relationship with Christ is what would have helped. But here I am on a level four maximum security prison; full of pain acting out living the same life style, often in trouble and in the hole, in bondage still serving the "S-god."

A while after I came to prison, my mother started going back to church; soon after my sisters also. They began to minister to me. I wasn't trying to hear it. I was serving the "S-god." I had all kinds of harsh things to say in my rebellion. My mother told me once that I made her feel like her relationship with Christ was all for nothing. I had caused my mother pain, so I held my tongue with her. My sister and I would always argue; our phone conversations always ended three ways:

1) My mother taking the phone

2) My sister calling me stupid

3) My sister talking to a dial tone

Soon after my mother found me a pen pal, a woman of God, and she soon started in on me as well. All alone, they were planting seeds in my life, and in the fullness of time God caused those seeds to blossom. Now the seeds are blossoming. I can't remember if it was a conversation that my mother and I had on the phone or in the visiting room, but here came Jesus. I told my mother (hoping to bring an end to the conversation), that if I was to say anyone was God, she was it... she was the one who put clothes on my back, a roof over my head and food on the table, so I don't believe in God, and if I do she is it. My mother told me, "I'm not God and please don't say that I am. I'm not ready to die." She went on to tell me, "God will knock down everything you set before him just to show you that he is God."

Keeping that in mind a short while later, I called home and couldn't reach anyone; so I called my Aunt Carol and she in turn made a call. The person who answered was sitting at a desk in a hospital, so she patched us through to my mother's room. I'm on the phone thinking, *what's wrong with my Pop's* until my Mom told me that it was her. Now that past conversation is replaying in my head, and I thought *I'm gonna kill my mother.* All along, she's telling me they think she may have had a mild stroke. They're not sure what happened, but they were coming in to examine her and could I call her back in 10 or 15 minutes.

Now keep in mind, I'm serving the "S-god"; the "S-god" couldn't do this one for me, he was powerless. I stood right there in Lancaster State Prison, D yard, building 5, next to phone 80, and said *Lord, if your will heal my mother, I will serve you for the rest of my life.*

I called back; my mother said, "Baby the doctor gave me a clean bill of health, I'll be home in 15 or 20 minutes; call me then."

A short time after that we had a convention in the visiting room, and I remember the Preacher saying three men were on the cross, two deserved to die, one didn't, but he did it anyway just for you. At that point, I opened up my mouth and asked Christ into my life, and asked him to be the Lord of my life. Since then I've truly been blessed and my life hasn't been the same, and it never will be again!

Christ is faithful, he's given me peace, a heart of flesh, forgiveness, and love and I now can love and forgive others as well as myself. Even in prison, the Lord has counted me worthy to be in the ministry. He's blessed me with a loving godly wife, and son (that friend/pen-pal my mother found), but God ordained it before the foundations of the world. He's given me the grace and strength to face life behind the wall! God is so good and faithful!!!!

Ephesians 1:3-4: Blessed be the God and Father of our Lord Jesus Christ, who have blessed us with all spiritual blessings in Heavenly places in Christ: according as he has chosen us in him before the foundation of the world that we should be holy and without blame before him in love.

Travielle James Craig – H-98882

Testimonial of Greg Sanders

I was born in 1956 on the East Side of Los Angeles, on 73rd between Hooper and Central Avenue to be specific. My generation was one of "respect," house parties and making love with our childhood sweethearts. We would always settle our disagreements with our fists and on extreme occasions with a "hook knife." I came up with Big Raymond Washington and Stanley "Tookie" Williams, two very strong and unique individuals that I had the pleasure and privilege of knowing; may both of their spirits rest in peace...

I can remember when we first started "Crippin" and what it truly meant to be a special part of something so new and exciting. I can remember how we all started saying "Crips don't die, we multiply"; and how it just caught on all of the East Side and soon beyond. It was the summer of 1969 and I was 13 years old. Raymond had elected himself as a dominating force who demanded respect. He got it!!

During the next five years, I was going back and forth between Church and the Hood. My parents were very strict and religious; I was compelled to go to Church and it made me very rebellious towards God and my parents. The next five years of my life were very hard and I found myself headed toward life in prison in 1979. I haven't been out since and my walk with Christ has truly intensified.

During these past 30 years, I've grown spiritually and I truly believe that I've made some positive changes for the better. I'm now a mature man of God, studying to show myself approved continually. I'm currently in the process of helping youngsters turn their life around and perhaps find the Lord for themselves.

God Bless,
Greg Sanders

Testimonial of Darell L. Flowers

My story begins as one like many young men who grew up in South Central Los Angeles. I was born in Little Rock, Arkansas and my mother and I moved to Los Angeles, California when I was three years old. My mother was very young when she gave birth to me only 14 years old and still a child herself. So I was basically a child of my grandmother. I still call her Mom to this day. I never had any brothers or sisters, just me so that made me sort of a loner. My mother started doing drugs at a very young age so I kind of raised myself in the streets. My father was back in Arkansas and he was never a big part of my life.

At age 14, I started looking for that father figure, so I joined a gang thinking that would ease my pain. My biological father was thousands of miles away and my mother was hooked on drugs, so I had to survive the best way I knew how, by any means. I started getting into all sorts of trouble and I lost a sense of respect for women, because my mother had abandoned me and it seemed as if she didn't love me either, so I then began disrespecting girls. Eventually as a result of gang banging, I got shot in my chest next to my heart and I almost died. I knew back then there was something or someone watching over my life, but I just couldn't put my finger on it at that point.

As the years went on, I continued in my street madness but never got caught up, so I thought I was untouchable; but still, there was something or someone who was watching over me guiding my steps. In 1995 after a series of unfortunate events that took place in my life, I decided to stop gang banging and take control of my life. I had two young kids and I needed to start being a father to them. I went back to school and got my G.E.D. Then, I got a job and things in my life seemed to finally start coming together.

But I had something that I was still holding on to: "disrespecting women". Later on down the line, this would really become a problem in my life to the point of my almost taking a woman's life. Now I sit in prison with a life sentence, but better days are sure to come.

Just when I thought I had everything together, I wasn't in control of anything. After my first two weeks of being incarcerated, I ran into an old gang member rival of mine. I couldn't even recognize this brother because it had been so long since I've been out of that life style; but he recognized me. In fact, he had some information for me that would soon change my whole life; Jesus Christ cleaned him up and gave him a real chance to have a life. This went on [he ministered to me] for several days and this Brother really had a testimony that penetrated my heart to accept Jesus Christ as my Lord and savior.

As time goes by now, I know what that something or someone that has been there with me watching and guiding my path for all these years; it was Jesus Christ. I haven't had an easy life and to this day I still struggle with certain temptations; but one thing I have come to understand is that God is faithful and his promises will come to pass. Now I know that my life is on that right path, my destiny is in God's hand, and my future will over shadow my past regrets and disappointments. God's love for us is unfathomable and his mercy and grace endures forever. Amen

God Bless You,

Bro. Obadiah

"Servant of the Lord"

Darell L. Flowers – F79845

Testimonial of Lamarr Cooks

I would like to share my testimony with those who will be reading this, and I pray that it comforts you, and puts you in a state of mind to want to change the way you may be living if it's not pleasing to the sight of God.

This was my life, before I came to Christ, and allowed him to take control of my life. At a very young age, in elementary school (4th and 5th grade) is when I began my life of crime. At that age, my crimes were stealing candy out of liquor stores, clothes out of shopping malls, and bicycles. At the age of 12, I started burglarizing homes and businesses. During all this time, I was getting up on Sunday and going to church with my mother and two brothers. At a young age, God was speaking to me but I just wouldn't listen. I believe he was trying to tell me something, about if I didn't stop the things I was doing, how my life would turn out. And don't think I wasn't getting caught committing these crimes. "You will Always Get Caught."

I got involved in a gang Front Street Crip. I started carrying guns, selling drugs, going in and out of juvenile halls, placement homes, and now at age 36, I am now serving a sentence of LIFE without parole, for a murder back in 1991. Only if I had listened to God, I wouldn't be in this situation.

Eight years into serving my time, the year 1999, God spoke to my spirit. In order to do that, he settled me down so he had my full attention. He began to show me a different way of living, with peace in my life and having a humbled heart. And it's not to say because I'm in jail that I want God in my life. It is where God has put me, to settle me down with no distractions of the world's fast lane of living.

I began to read my Bible and watch the Christian station on my TV. I began a daily routine of praying constantly and that's when God began working through me, giving me a different way of thinking, how I felt towards other people and the way I used to live. Peace began to overwhelm my heart to where I had no fear of anything, because I knew God had my back. I began to have no love for the way I used to live, because I knew people got hurt, whether [they were] victims of my crimes or my family for dealing with me, in and out of incarceration.

Now, when I first gave myself to Christ, it wasn't easy, because don't forget Satan is real and is out to destroy your life as much as he can. So I struggled through a couple of years, until I got around some Christian Brothers (Inmates) who pushed me into staying positive, got me into church and got me baptized in 2007. God has been so good to me. In my life without him, I would still be caught up in using drugs, running with the gangs and just having a negative attitude towards life.

Since my incarceration, and allowing God Almighty to control my life, I have obtained my G.E.D., a vocational trade and am now working on receiving my AA Degree in college. Serving God, he will surround you with positive people and positive things. Trust him; God will not disappoint you, "Man will."

In Psalms 32:8 it says "I will instruct you and teach you in the way you should go; I will guide you with my eye.

Don't be like me and not listen to GOD when he's trying to get your attention. His word is truth. The devil is a liar so we need to give up our way of living and live for Christ who died for our sins so we may have eternal life with him: II Corinthians 5:15.

My last words to you are from the Bible God says in John14:27

HEAVEN OR HELL

Peace I leave with you, my peace I give to you and not as the world gives do I give to you. Let not your heart be troubled, but neither let it be afraid.

In Jesus' name,

Lamarr Cooks

H88770

Testimonial of Kenneth Underwood

I am 30 years old; I was born and raised in Los Angeles, California, mainly residing in Watts. I have always seen and heard a lot of good and bad things!

I remember when I was about eight years old; I was very young and curious. I was always looking for something new and different to get into. So I started to pay attention to my older brother and father, who were heavily involved in gangs, guns, and drugs. By that time, I was already making gang signs with my little fingers, and claiming the neighborhood my older brother was claiming, which was the Nut Hood Watts Crips.

Living a life that consisted of such violence and negativity wasn't so easy. As I started to grow in the gang life being easily influenced by those around me, I became more involved in criminal activities.

By the time I was 12 years old, I started selling drugs to earn extra money, and once I seen [saw] that I could benefit from selling someone a little white rock, I started to do it more often. I became more submerged in the life of gang banging and selling drugs. I fell in love with it! By the time I was 13 years old, I was doing what I felt most kids did that were raised in Watts, California, which was gangbang and sell drugs. I felt like I was doing what I was born to do!

At the age of 19, I found myself standing before a Judge, looking at time in prison for a residential burglary. I went to jail and didn't get out until I was 21, a week and a half before my 22nd birthday.

One would have thought after my first experience with the California State Prison System that I would have learned my lesson. However, I did end up being incarcerated again. After going through so much in jail, I finally decided to change my life! I began attending

Church services and reading my Bible. Automatically, I began to become renewed in my mind, my speech changed. I even stopped gang banging and behaved differently than I use to. So now, here I stand, a changed man who started off as a troubled young man.

One of the main reasons I became a better person is because of God and his Son, Jesus Christ. I share my testimony with you to bring to your attention that from experience, it's a life that no one else should want to go through. Now that I am older, I can see where I went wrong. I've been there, I've done that and I've lived that, and I'll never go back.

If you're living the life of gang banging, using and selling drugs, please be encouraged to change.

Yours Truly,

Underwood, K.

AA-6288

Testimonial of Odell Hale, Jr.

As I reflect back on my journey through life and the hood experiences that served to mold and shape my character, there was nothing visible in my personality, or projected in the goals, that I sought to achieve that would have suggested that I as a man who would become a dedicated disciple of Jesus Christ.

Though originally from Cincinnati, Ohio, my family migrated to Los Angeles California in 1963. Due to poverty, and large family of (seven) siblings, my parents were compelled to establish residence in some low-income projects in Watts.

Shortly after moving to Watts, I became acquainted with some kids, who were street wise because of their poor living conditions. They were compelled to develop a hustle, "some mack'd for acquiring fast money." My country boy mentality didn't have a suitable place in this environment, so after some grooming and coaching by my street life associations, I transformed from an innocent country boy to a street living, liquor consuming, weed smoking, girl chasing, gun packing, and money craving hustler. I was held in bondage of this life style by the devil's promise of prosperity, if I remained dedicated to his cause. I became what is labeled a "state raised baby," which in essence is a person who's been recognized for the extensive time he or she spent going in and out of institutions.

Along with the aging process, maturity came and the realization that my life was being wasted. I became worn and torn inside, and at the end of myself, weariness had begun to take its toll. I really didn't know what it was going to take or where to look for whatever it was that my life was lacking, but God did. He sent me an Angel in the form of an ex-gang member, who now stood in the gap for me. And so this Brother offered me a life altering solution. The Brother in Christ presented me with the gospel message of salvation I had in Jesus Christ. So I opened up the door to my heart and let Jesus in. He lifted me up out of a horrible pit, out of the miry clay, set my feet up upon a Rock and established my steps. There is nothing that makes a fall more significant than a strong stance constructed by Jesus.

Your Brother in Christ,

O'Dell Hale Jr.

#F16300

Testimonial of Brother Maurice

PRAISE THE LORD!!!

My name is Brother Maurice Hastings, but some know me as Brother Moe. My journey started long ago, when I was a young boy. I grew up in the streets of Los Angeles, on the East Side. I was not an original resident of Los Angeles; I came to Los Angeles when I was 7 years old. At that time, we had a small family, my Dad and Mom, two sisters and a one month old baby brother. Things started to go downhill when my Dad and Mom separated. With only my Mom to supervise and raise me, I started to venture into the streets. With two sisters at home, there was no male figure around.

There was a young boy, my age that I met; his name was Alfred, and everyone called him Nugget. Nugget was my homeboy for years to come. Nugget and I hung out with about two or three other homies and they became my family away from my other family. As years passed, all of us stayed close friends; we even went to the same school. We began to get into trouble together, and eventually we started gangbanging. The gang life was a hard and rough life. I didn't care about life and I didn't care about death.

My mother was always praying for me; she used to tell me that she was afraid that someone would call her and inform her I was in the streets dead. I didn't know at the time, but God had his hand on my life.

As I continued in rebellion, I was arrested at the age of 16 for murder and sent to C.Y.A., for a number of years. When I was released from C.Y.A., my rebellion continued, and the gangbanging continued. Along the way during that time, several adults would try to tell me about God, and about how much he loved me. But I wasn't listening.

I was arrested again, and this time I was sent to State Prison for 6 to 20 years. I was only 19 years old. My trials continued even in prison. I ended up in the hole and the shu for about a year. After I got out of the hole, I settled back into prison life. I didn't know at the time, but God was still trying to get my attention, and to show himself real and true to me. I wasn't sure if there *was* a God that loved me like people would say.

One day in prison, I decided to attend church. I thought I would attend church and convince the authorities there that I had changed, hoping to receive a parole date. I attended services the first time; I didn't participate in what was going on, and I just sat there during the service. The next time I attended, I sat there a little bored and decided to pray. I didn't know how to pray, I didn't even know if God was real! I prayed: *God if you are real, I want to go home one day soon.* That's all I said, and one month after I prayed that prayer the laws changed, and a new law started. I was over sentenced; I was released from prison and forgot about God.

He showed me that he was real, but my rebellion continued. I started selling drugs and doing other illegal activities for financial gain. As the years passed, I started exploiting women sexually and financially through boosting and pandering. In my rebellion, I hurt people, and destroyed lives. That's was the only way I knew how to live.

I left California and moved to Pittsburgh PA; there I continued to live the street life. I prospered above average financially, but still I had neither peace nor happiness. In Pittsburgh, I had a very close friend name Reggie. Reggie was a pimp from Buffalo, New York. He had a girlfriend that worked the streets for him named Adrienne. Adrienne and I became good friends. She was using drugs one day and had a very bad experience. I didn't see her for a year, and when I did, she had given her life to Christ. Every time I would see her, she and her Christian friends would be sharing Christ. God was using her to get my attention.

But at times I would see her from a distance and hide from her or go the other way. I was still running from God. After a year or so, I went back to California to visit my family and some friends. I visited for 15 to 20 days and returned to Pittsburgh PA. After I was there about two weeks, my family informed me that the authorities were looking for me for murder. I left Pittsburgh and returned to Los Angeles only to reunite with my old homies, the East Coast Crip Gang. From there my life continued. Back to selling drugs. I was finally arrested for the murder I was being sought for.

At that time, I was sick and tired, and disappointed. All my life I had dedicated my time to gangs, and the street life. I was tired of being sick and tired of no peace, no joy, and no happiness! Here I was in jail with nothing. I thought about all the people that God sent into my life, all the time. I would run from his call, as I sat in the county jail awaiting trial, I received a Bible. I would read it every day. I read Matthew 11:28, 29, 30 where it says, "Come unto me, all you that labor and are heavy laden, and I will give you rest. Take my yoke upon you and learn of me; for I am meek and lowly in heart, and you shall find rest unto your souls, for my yoke is easy and my burden is light."

I also read in John 10:10 that "the thief cometh not, but for to steal, and to kill, and to destroy, I am come that they might have life, and that they might have it more abundantly." I was tired; I wanted that rest that Jesus was talking about. I wanted that abundant life he spoke of. One night I became very serious with God, there in my cell. I asked Christ to come into my life and forgive me for all I had done, all the hurt I had caused, and the lives I had destroyed. I was very sincere. I meant business.

Since that time, God has really changed my life, and given me a new beginning. Even though I'm still incarcerated, and serving a life sentence, I have all the peace and joy that I never had in my life living for the world. I'm allowing God to use me right where I am.

I wanted to encourage you today, give your life to Jesus Christ. The Bible says in Romans 3:23 that "all have sinned, and come short of the glory of God."

Romans 3:10 says "there is none righteous, no, and not one." The Bible also says, "For the wages of sin is death; but the gift of God is eternal life through Jesus Christ our Lord." No matter how your life is, God will give you a new beginning. Trust him today!!

Brother in Christ!!

Brother Maurice

Job 23:10

Testimonial of Dortell Williams

I was that guy down the way who was slicker than the slickest, or so I thought. I was that guy who put the slick in oil, or so I thought. Yeah, I was the guy who was slicker than wet wax . . . or so I thought. And such was the life of deception, for I know, I was the one deceived.

So I cheated credit card companies, stole cars, sold drugs and exploited the addictions of hapless others; callously robbing them of their freedom, their families, and the abundant life Jesus intended for them to have. Yet, I, myself, was a mere pawn for the devil that used me – and so many others like me – to advance his mission to steal, kill and destroy.

Still, God had his eye on me, calling me away from a life of deception and into a life of truth. First, my cohort in criminality, Eric, flipped out and arrived at my door one Sunday; suited up, with a black-leather-bound bible clutched in his right hand, inviting me to church.

Rapt in ignorance and arrogance, I laughed at Eric, thinking I was clowning him, yet rejecting the very maker of the universe, Yahweh, Himself. God's mystifying mercy continued in my foolish footpaths, this time through my stepmother, Anna, just a few short weeks later.

Responding to an invite to a pool party at Anna's in Compton, on Essey Street, I was zealously gratifying my flesh with food and drink. Anna ever so lovingly pulled me to one side and for no apparent reason whispered sternly in my ear: "I don't know what you're doing wrong, but whatever it is you need to stop and come to the Lord."

I noted it, gazed into her onyx-colored eyes for a moment, taking in the sincerity, and nodded respectfully with a smile. I walked away unheeding, into a life of full-fledged sin.

Life's fast lane ushered me along with secular obligations that in retrospect were like a hammer's wheel that kept me vainly moving, but took me nowhere. I ping-ponged my way from city to city and remorselessly distributed my street-level pharmaceutical poison. I stroked my salivating ego with female conquests who were probably more interested in the contents of my pockets than the contents of my personality.

Finally, just days before my life would come to a screeching tragic derailment; I heard a clear audible voice from within tell me, "This is it. You need to stop." I ignored it, it turned out to be the poorest of every decision I'd ever made. Shortly thereafter, my beautiful, young wife of two years was shot during one of my illegal transactions and I was held criminally accountable for her death.

It wasn't until I found myself at wit's end; until I realized by reading the testimonies of the saved in a Godly magazine that I understood I was lost, and that God wanted to put blessed, eternal claims on my life.

It was October 17, 1989, that I knelt on my humble knees in that cold, cramped Hall-of Justice, Los Angeles County Jail cell, and surrendered my life to my Savior, Jesus Christ.

I haven't looked back since, except to laugh at myself, and my own ignorance and arrogance; like I did when my ole cohort in criminality showed up at my door inviting me to church back in the day. Only this time I knew the laugh was on me.

Still, my days have been blessed beyond anything I could ever have imagined, even in this chaos-laden world of confinement. I finally learned that the riches I was so vigorously chasing in the material world are far more superior in the spiritual. Think about it … I had to come to prison to find salvation and peace. What a trip of ignorance and arrogance to learn that God truly does work in mysterious ways.

BIO

Dortell Williams is a forty-three year old freelance writer. He is currently taking a correspondence course to earn an Associate of Arts degree. He has taught himself Spanish and has been published by the Christian Science Monitor, the Final Call, and the San Francisco Bay View newspapers, to name a few.

Testimonial of Virgil Clark

I guess I can start my testimony at age 13, a year after I came to California. I can tell you I seriously didn't want to be here. Even though many fun things have happened in my life, I still didn't want to be here. You see, originally I'm from Philadelphia, Pennsylvania; there I was on my own stomping grounds. Here it was all strange to me, and I hated it. That hatred steadily grew until I didn't recognize myself any longer. I started to feel dark and crazy for reasons I couldn't grasp. That was the beginning of my downfall; but I couldn't see it.

I've made my share of mistakes in High School trying to be down with the "in-crowd." I kidded myself into thinking that I didn't care about being popular. But when I became popular, I would do anything to remain that way.

The biggest mistake I've ever made was perhaps a blessing in disguise. I say that because when I came to jail, that is where my life was saved. The circumstances surrounding my case are tragic and I will forever regret how my actions led to an innocent woman's death; as a result, I am serving a life sentence. The bright side to the whole situation is that, I have found God and I've learned the truth about God's word. See, God will call his people out of the strangest places. Some can be hated enemies such as the KKK's, Skinheads, SUR13, BGF's, and Black Panthers, or any other group. Point is it doesn't matter what worldly title you gave yourself. When God calls you, all the racial hatred you feel will fade away.

Look at Saul, who's now known as Paul. When he heard Jesus' voice he immediately turned from persecuting (God's) people, started spreading the gospel and became Paul. Many people are being saved today and will be in the future. I've learned that the more you harden your heart to God's gentle call, the harder your fall will be. It doesn't matter how big you are in your own eyes, you will suffer a big fall, and then you will finally understand and hear God. I had to have my freedom stripped from me; and then while locked up, I had to hit rock bottom, before I finally listened to God's voice.

When I was at SATF/SP, I started to read God's word; but I really didn't understand it. So God saw fit to place me on a yard at Lancaster State Prison, where I could get materials that I needed to understand what God was saying to me. Through his word, not to mention the Brothers' he surrounded me with who helped me see and study instead of just read, God chose me, and I'm so ecstatic that he did. God has truly worked a miracle in my life. I give all praise to God.

Virgil Jason Clarke

J92139

Testimonial of Maelon Niblett

I was brought up in a house with both parents, including an older brother. My parents have always believed in God, but are not practicing Christians.

I took to the streets and became addicted to that life, addicted to doing wrong. I clowned around in school, robbed people and stole from passersby. If it was wrong, I was involved.

I ended up going to prison when I was only 19 years old. I was busted for robbery and using drugs. I regained my freedom and managed to avoid the long arm of the law for eight years. During that time, I met my lovely wife. She gave me a healthy, beautiful child, a girl.

Still, I was not happy with my lifestyle. I was still using and selling drugs, playing a field of women and drinking a private river of alcohol. From light drugs to heavy narcotics, I graduated to jumping on and beating my wife. I was again arrested, tried and convicted … sent to prison where I remain today.

During my time in the county jail, going through the court process, a neighbor inside brought me a Bible to read. That was 14 years ago.

I began reading it. I read it daily with growing enthusiasm. The truth shined brightly before me and I began to see what I was missing, where I went wrong.

While there are an abundance of drugs and alcohol to be had inside (prison), God removed the desire from me for these things. God also returned my wife to me. We share a much deeper and more meaningful relationship now than ever. Based on the foundation of God, we were formally married.

Since I accepted God into my life, he has given me purpose, direction, clarity of mind and wisdom to avoid the foolishness of my past.

I am truly thankful for God's Grace!

Maelon Niblett

Testimonial of Hamid Zadeh

I was a sinner but did not know it. I thought that if I gave to charity, prayed more and fasted, I would be covered. I thought that this was enough. I thought I was with God. I did not know better. I was a religious person, following man's doctrine and spiritually dead. I did not know that I was far from the way of truth. I did not know God. I was 180 degrees opposite of the way of the Lord. I thought I was walking in the right way and I loved God. But I was walking in Satan's way and in the way of the world and man.

I was born in a Muslim country and I became Muslim. I grew up in a religious family. In my heart, there was no room for the Spirit of Forgiveness and the true love of the Lord. I did not understand the spiritual word of God, of His Kingdom, at all.

I had a successful earthly life. Then, at the age of 42, I was arrested and put in prison for life without parole. I did not know that the true word existed in the Bible: Proverbs 3: 11-12 and Roman 8:28.

At the age of 50 while in prison by the will of God, a Christian visited me and introduced me to the Lord Jesus Christ, and the true Word of God. Because I was not ready and not prepared, every time I read the Bible, I did not understand it at all (Acts8:30-31). This same Christian advised me, "Any time you want to pray, whatever you need, ask for it in the name of Jesus Christ." So, for the first time I did this. In all of my Muslim prayers, praying and fasting at the end, I asked God to grant my petition in the name of Jesus Christ. I also asked God to send someone to help me and teach me his spiritual understanding, his word, until I became close to him (Matthew 6:33 and Matthew 7:7-8).

After seven months from the first visit of this Christian, I saw a fellow prisoner, David, sitting alone reading his Bible. I asked him if he had time to answer some of my questions. He said that he could only give me an explanation and that for me to understand the Word of God was out of his hands. He said that it was in the authority of God and that if I was prepared, God would see this and give me understanding of his Word and that he would show me things as I grew.

For three weeks, I visited David every day. All day long, I asked him about the Word of God and about Jesus and God; and he explained them to me showing me verse by verse in the Bible.

After the weeks passed, I asked him to teach me the gospel. He answered, "I can only give you an explanation. If you walk in his righteous way, God will teach you his Spiritual Word." We started in the Gospel of Matthew after three months. David answered all of my questions with the Bible and showed me the right words. During this period, I truly repented. I remember one day that I was crying hard from the bottom of my heart. Tears came from my eyes like rain from a spring cloud. I asked God to accept my repentance and in the name of the Lord Jesus Christ to forgive me for all the years that I had been far from him and was a sinner (Roman 6: 6 and Hebrew 1:3).

The morning after we completed Matthew, I was praying and suddenly I understood several spiritual truths that I had not understood before and for the first time I understood the Lord Jesus Christ. It was as if I could see for the first time. I was healed by Christ and he gave me spiritual eyes. I realized that I had been blind before.

We began reading through the Gospel of Mark and Luke and continued through the Bible. I do not remember when or how I stopped praying in the Muslim way; I no longer fasted the way

Muslims do nor read the Quran. Now by the grace of God, I have a new understanding of the spiritual meaning of the Word of God; I have truly repented and have become a new person. I have been reborn in the spirit of Jesus Christ (John: 3:3; Luke 8:17-18; Ephesians 1:18).

On August 20, 2006, I was baptized by Pastor John in the prison chapel. Muslim prisoners were aware of my Christian baptism. That night, one of them dropped a letter in my cell and threatened me with death. The next day, I added two hours to my Bible study with Brother David out in the yard and made myself available for any Muslim that might want to see me; but none of them approached me (Joshua 1:5-9, Isaiah 41: 8-10, and Roman 8:31).

One day I was with Brother David reading the Book of Revelation. Suddenly a voice spoke into my ear and told me to read John 14:14-17 and that I would find my answer. Immediately I read those verses and was very happy to find that Holy Spirit dwells in my heart and mind. The Lord God honored me, accepted my repentance, chose me, cleansed and purified me from my sins. He took me into his house and called me His son (Isaiah 66:1-2, Ephesians: 2:21 and Luke 15:24). For one and a half years, I studied every day with Brother David. I finished both the New and the Old Testaments (Philippians 4:13).

In 2007, I began sharing the Word of God with other prisoners in the name of our Lord Jesus Christ. We now have a small group of spiritual Christians (John 6:44).

I asked God to use me by his will and to give me the honor of working for him, to help me to grow in the Spirit of the Lord Jesus Christ. I also asked him to help me by His Word and His Spirit to guide those who are in darkness and bring them to the light of truth through Jesus Christ into his kingdom; to reveal to them his Spiritual Word and to save them from Satan.

My passion is to share his Spiritual Word with those who are hungry and thirsty for the Kingdom of our Lord and God. I will tell them how beautiful and powerful his kingdom is; just as I am saved, they will be saved also.

In March 2009, the Holy Spirit guided me to start translating the English language Kings James Version Bible into Farsi. I started with Matthew, and on June 10, 2010, I finished all books. I hope that one day all people will come into the way of the Lord Jesus Christ and that all will speak the spiritual language with one Spirit (Galatians 2:20, John 14:20).

The year 2010 was my 13th year in prison. I have faith in the Word of God. I'm sure that just as Lord Jesus Christ saved my spirit by the will of our Father God, he will also take care of my body and bring justice to my case in his time (Matthew 28:19-20, Ezekiel 12:26-28 and Isaiah 40:25).

If any person has a desire to truly repent and return to the righteous way of the Lord, they must be guided and become spiritually free from the bondage of darkness, ignorance and sin. They must accept Jesus Christ as their Lord and Savior.

Hamid Zadeh

Testimonial of Donald E. Mitchell

As a child at a very young age, I became disobedient. I then started making a series of bad choices. I started to hang around gang members. My new name became "TRAY 8." I began to use and sell drugs. Soon the drugs got the best of me; I had a lot of hurt and anger that I carried around. I hurt a lot of people. I brought shame on my family over a series of bad choices I made. I lost a lot of friends over the foolishness I was involved in.

After years of living a life of negativity, I became weary. I was tired of living a life of deception. I wanted to get my life on a positive path; but I had to realize my faults and transgressions. Now by God's wonderful grace I am found. I am the first to admit that still I struggle. BUT, I learned God will not give you more that you can handle. Now I live sober and God is now my comfort, I found peace in Jesus Christ.

Take this sound advice from me, someone who knows from experience it ain't cool to sell drugs or use drugs. It's not cool to join a gang; it's a life of wickedness that will lead to DEATH or LIFE in prison. Please depart from evil while you still have the chance.

Sincerely,

Mr. Donald E. Mitchell

E75646

Testimonial of Hamilton Green

This testimonial I pray will reach and touch the lives of many. My hope is renewed through the grace and mercy of God the Father daily. I wholeheartedly stand firm in the faith given to me from God and our Lord and Savior Jesus Christ.

I was born and raised in South Central Los Angeles, in a loving home by my parents who brought up nine children in the admonition of the Lord (Proverbs 22:6). As I got into my teenage years, I was given freedom to make decisions outside the home.

There were pressures in my neighborhood that I chose to follow, which led me down the wrong path. I rebelled against my faith in Christ and lived in a backslidden condition from about the age of 14 until my mid 20's. My everyday life was surrounded with crimes. I committed everything from selling drugs to hurting people with violence out in the streets and being tied into the gang life. It turned my heart away from the true family values, which were taught in our household and I took to the norms of the street life.

During the years where I lived according to the code of a gangster, my everyday life was filled with danger; always looking for ways to make money illegally in any way I could. My most successful way was when I started selling cocaine. I truly thought it was better than robbing and stealing because the potential of hurting people violently wasn't there. But I soon found out that that aspect rose to a higher level!!

In the early 80's in South Central Los Angeles, there was a drug war of epic proportion! Many of the gangs held neighborhoods captive and the residents in fear of their safety. They fell victim to the lawlessness we lived by. This life-style led me to making a truly horrible decision, which landed me in prison with a life without parole sentence. However, I know that my life has a greater meaning because through it all, when I was out on the streets living a vile and wicked life, God still loved me.

What the devil meant to be bad, God turned for good! The enemy tried to take my life in 1986-87. I was on my deathbed twice, stabbed an inch from my heart; a year later shot in the stomach. Yet after being delivered through all that, I still ran, living a sin-filled life; but God allowed me this marvelous grace by letting me come to prison and by getting my full attention!

In early 1994 after about six years of still living a sinful life here in prison, the call of God weighed heavily on my life. Everything that was going on kept me in danger at every turn. Situations that arose were geared toward destroying my life! But I remembered what God's word says; "That those who call on the Lord shall be saved!" So one night while sitting in an eight by six by ten-foot cell alone, I called on the Lord to save me from my sinful nature and the life I was living; and from that night, I never looked back. Through much prayer and supplication, I kept myself in the word of God. Willfully doing his will by obeying the statutes and ordinances in spirit and in truth, I now run the race, which is set before me gladly!

The Lord truly works in our lives even if we can't see it, and I know now looking back, that when we're chosen of God, he will finish that work he started in us!! As I look back now, I know there many who've taken the same path and weren't spared like I was; but when the call of God is on your life, don't run from it as Jonah did (Jonah 1:3). Make the biggest decision of your "LIFE," the best one, by confessing you're a sinner, and that you need the Savior. "The Lord Jesus Christ"

Hebrews 12:1 Wherefore seeing we also are compassed about with so great a cloud of witnesses, let us lay aside every weight, and the sin which doeth that so easily besets us, let us run with patience the race that is set before us.

Brother Hamilton W. Green

Testimonial of Averial Alexander

I was born and raised in Southeast, Los Angeles. When I was about 3 years old, my Grandmother took me in, due to my being abandoned by my mother. My Dad passed away when I was six years old. It took a toll on me, not having my parents in my life. I didn't know what I wanted to do, even though my Grandmother was trying her hardest to raise me. I was taking things for granted, not realizing who I was, who I could be if I put my all into it, and stopped blaming my mistakes on somebody else. When I should have taken responsibility for my own actions, I was hard headed thinking I knew it all; but to keep it truthful I didn't know anything. Talk is cheap but my actions were not speaking louder than words. I've hurt a lot of people who cared so much about me. Sometimes I wondered why I was doing those things, but I didn't have an explanation of why. Then one day, something touched me and told me to try something new.

I started preaching the word of God at an early age. I preached at different Churches, such as, Second Mount Olive, Christ Full Gospel, True Love Baptist Church and a few others. I thought I knew God; but I didn't know you could know his word and not know God. I realized what I was doing; I was playing with God, not taking God seriously. Then I didn't know what to do with myself, I didn't know which way to turn.

So I joined 118 East Coast Block Crip Gang, trying to fit in and be something that I wasn't put on this earth to be. The money, the females, the guns and everything that came with gang banging at the time seemed cool but all along, it was stupid on my behalf. I was doing stuff that I didn't have to do. I thought the homies cared. The only thing they cared about was themselves, and everything I did for the hood was for nothing, I mean for nothing.

I got 37 years with 85 percent for nothing. But to think about it I'm glad I went through all this. All it did was open my eyes to reality, and made me realize all the stuff my Grandmother was telling me was the stone cold truth. If I was blinded to her love then, I know now her love was totally real. Real as in, God is good; his mercy endures forever.

Now my Grandmother has passed away, I got to live right, as she looks over me I got to be the best I can be and take life seriously because life ain't no game and it's never too late to learn. My name is Averial Alexander, not some thug; I'm a human being. I love myself; that was the first step of changing my life. No one owes me or anybody else anything. I had to snap out the games. Because we all got to live our life like it's the last day.

We all got struggles and problems but everything happens for a reason. You wouldn't know God was able to fix your problem or struggles unless you had them. If everything was perfect, we wouldn't need God. I put God in front of everything I do, I'm not a child any more, I'm a man. I can't live in the past any more. I got to live in the present and be that man that I would want my child to be. I'm not perfect and I'm not about to pretend that I am. I was called to preach the word and help others get closer to God, because we all need to get closer to him, the Almighty. I love the Lord he heard my cry. Amazing Grace how sweet the sound, I once was lost but now I'm found and I believe that

I can do all things through Christ who strengthen me. Philippians 4:13

Averial Alexander

F42195

Testimonial of R. Chapman

Before I found the Lord, my life consisted of negative ambitions, evil thoughts and complete ignorance of where my life was headed.

Rightfully so, I got arrested on January 5, 2007, on numerous felony charges, and I faced three life sentences. You would think that I've learned my lesson, right.

Wrong, I still indulged in my sinful ways, for I was comfortable in my sins. One of the biggest steps you can take is changing. For without change, I would still been in my corrupted ways.

So God stepped in, in the most subtle of ways. I started going to school and found school wasn't so bad. I'm still incarcerated to this day, but at that particular time, I was in Sylmar Juvenile Hall.

Then I started to find out that obtaining knowledge was fulfilling. Over a certain period of time, I came to recognize that there must be more to life than life itself.

So I decided to evaluate the knowledge I was obtaining. (In a worldly sense, it was positive). I came to realize it was vain in a selfish way because it couldn't satisfy curiosity. It couldn't answer my questions. So ultimately, I was led to the word of God, despite what others thought about how ridiculous it was.

God has shown me amazing truths. Now I see just how deceptive the world can be. Upon me giving a testimony, I must not withhold what the Lord has done for me. Upon me getting Baptized on July 4, 2009; God has not only showed me how Satan operates, but where he's now operating. Before I leave off with a final note, anybody who is blessed to see can see what God will show you.

Our main focus should be on, "Thus said the Lord." Investigate the claims of ministers, preachers, pastors. Satisfy you curiosity. Have your questions answered, for we must work out our own salvation. Have in your thoughts: does it align with what God said? (There's nothing wrong with having skepticism when you hear God's word. Your skepticism should lead you to search for the truth. Do research!!)

And remember, God will never disappoint you when it comes to the truth. Walk in integrity, have an honest approach and may God Bless you who are willing to sacrifice self for God's sake.

Romans 12:1: I beseech you therefore, Brethren, by the mercies of God, that you present your bodies a living sacrifice, Holy, Acceptable unto God, which is your reasonable service.

R. Chapman

Testimonial of DeAngelo McVay

My name is DeAngelo McVay, and I would like to share my before and after life. Before I was saved, I was living deep in sin, chasing women, drinking and selling tons of drugs.

I knew there was a God and I thought one day that I could just stop doing everything on my own. I also thought that when I stopped doing all those things, I would go to heaven, not knowing that I could have died in my sin.

No one ever told me I had to repent with a sincere heart and ask Jesus to come into my heart, forgive me of my sin, even though I had been baptized and was once in the church choir. Well, when I came to jail, I thought I would call on God since I had seen my mother and my kids' Grandma always calling on God. God seemed to always deliver them, so I thought, now is the time to call on him in my time of trouble.

So I did just that and nothing happened, until I talked to my mother on the phone one day. She told me to stop playing around with God. She told me that I could fool her or other people, but I couldn't fool God; "he knows all things so don't lie, Son."

I remember when I went back into my cell and later on that day, it weighed heavy on my heart. That night, Rev. Anthony came in and preached a sermon on how to be saved. Then he went on further and sang "Amazing Grace," and it seemed like my whole heart was shattered. I started crying and that's when I gave my life over to God with a sincere heart. But I must say that the picture of God's salvation plan didn't become clear to me until I started reading the Bible on my own. I had tried every road there was to take for happiness, peace, joy, love and all the above.

But when God, the author and finisher of my life came into my heart and changed my whole life, I knew this was the way. I was there when Jesus turned the light on; it was just as the song goes...

"Amazing Grace, How Sweet the sound that saved a wretch like me"

DeAngelo McVay

Testimonial of Keith Littlefield

For virtually 25 years now, prison has been the extent of my life experience. This is due in large part, to some very bad decisions I made as a youth growing up, which resulted in my incarceration. My life as a youth was one characterized by willful rebellion, manifested through the destructive terrain of gang banging and all that accompanied such a lifestyle-causing hurt to my family and the community that surrounded me. Selfish, I saw life through the myopic scopes of pride, and this supposed sense of invincibility, where all that mattered was me, and the maintenance of my own internal insecurities.

At the age of 18, I was arrested and charged with second-degree murder, and subsequently sentenced to 17 years to life in prison. Much to my shame and regret, I expressed this and accepted full responsibility for it.

These years of incarceration, and after having come to the end of myself, I began to take an honest and courageous inventory of myself. Thus, I came to realize the futility of where my life has led all these years epitomized by gangs, and the emptiness that such a life is imminently conducive to, and I began to see that within me a change was needed.

As time progressed, I was privileged to hear the testimonies of some men whose lives demonstrated the power of what GOD can do in the most undeserved of man. Hearing the plan of salvation through these men, that GOD has for every man and woman who's willing to repent of their past sins, and to turn to GOD by receiving Christ Jesus as their Lord and Savior, and through this confession unto salvation, you are born again.

Moved by the poignancy of GOD's plan of salvation available to me, several weeks later, I, by the grace of GOD received Christ as my Lord and Savior. I stand today a new man, whose life is hidden with Christ in GOD.

Though physically confined, the Blood of Jesus has freed me, from the shackles of my past, from the paralysis of my mistakes that by faith in Christ I live seeking only, that which is good and that which glorifies GOD.

There's no greater honor and privilege than to have rest in GOD through Christ Jesus, and no greater motivation than to receive the life he has for me.

Truly, I am thankful to Christ, for without him where would I be.

In Christ,

Keith Littlefield

D13509

Testimonial of G. English

"The Life"

The life of crime is like a roller coaster ride; it starts out fun, fast and flies.... Yeah right!!

Thirty years later, I'm still doing a life sentence inside of a maximum-security prison in California, for First Degree MURDER/187. Take it from me an Ex-Crook, Insane E.

The "life" of crime is a TRAP!! An evil trap!! Like those before and those who blindly continue to stumble down this dead end street will know too late, there ain't no future in being a CROOK! You might escape the law for a while, but sooner or later you're going to fall. And all the money, cars, jewelry, clothes and apartments or homes will all be like a canceled check . . . Gone. These words come from a mellowed black man who has had to navigate and stand tall through this maze of madness behind prison walls for 3-decades. It sure ain't been fun, it definitely hasn't gone by fast, and there really isn't anything fly about doing time. Surrounded by mentally ill, fake want to be gangsters in here (in prison), you should think long and hard about the consequences of that "Life" of crime.

What I've come to know as the truth, is getting right with GOD the Creator of each and every one of us. About 10 years ago, I found myself in "The Hole" for the same hustling: "The LIFE." What was different that time was that I was coming to understand and clearly see how much I was disgusted and tired of this sea of negativity, living that lifestyle of drugs, violence, retaliation, and rolling with the crew.

Finally, I had the good sense while in that stripped cage (the hole), freezing my butt off in nothing but my T-shirt and boxer shorts. I told myself: *this really ain't cool. I'm sick of this lifestyle.* I kneeled down and prayed. I asked God to change my heart and desire for that lifestyle. I prayed every day and shed tears of pain; my heart heard and I felt at ease. Calmness came over me and I told God that I wasn't going to be misled by the devil any longer. I said *God help me get right and change!!!*

As I continued to pray every day, and talk with GOD, I began feeling peace within that only God can give us! It felt like all this weight lifted up off me. In its place was a feeling and sense of peace. I've continued to talk and pray to God the Creator of us all every day since. It was made clear that God had been calling me to him. But being caught up in "THE LIFE" of crime is a distraction and mental disturbance from our true relationship with God. The "LIFE" of crime ain't nothing but a "DEAD-END STREET".

Today I'm strong in the Lord Jesus Christ my true friend! I'm so glad I came to the Lord Jesus Christ. The daily reading of my bible is now a joy for me.

Philippians 3: 13: Brother I count not myself to have apprehended: but this one thing I do, forgetting those things which are behind, and reaching forth unto those things which are before.

Philippians 4:13: I can do all things through Christ who strengthen me.

Brother G. English

C19699

Summation

I hope after reading this, it will bring a better understanding for parents, caregivers and youth, as to why someone chooses to join a gang, sell and use drugs, and/or other unsavory things. Everyone in this book started out as innocent child and at some point that innocence was stolen by the tricks of the devil. Most grew up in unfavorable circumstances where they let events that had happened in their lives harden their hearts, and give them an "I don't care" mentality. Some have been emotionally abandoned by their parents or other family members and society in general.

They have made mistakes that they now have learned to regret through the Love, and Grace of God. Where they once didn't care about another living soul, they now have compassion and a general concern for the youth of today. Now, in attempt to save the youth of today from their mistakes, they are reaching out to the world to prevent others from following in their footsteps.

After reading this, you should feel compelled to reach out also; to at risk youth and any person that has lost their way. This book is a demonstration of Gods Work. No matter where you are, if you call on him with repentance for your sins and a sincere heart; if you ask him to enter in and take control of your life, and then allow him to do just that, "HE WILL"!!

INDIVIDUAL STUDY QUESTIONS

The purpose of these questions is to help you reflect on your past, present and future.

When answering these questions, be transparent with yourself and or your support group. When you fail to be totally honest in this process, even about things you may not want to admit or share, you are continuing to hinder yourself from getting the help you need. This is the only way you can truly confront your past and move forward.

The truth you reveal can help you save your own life as well as someone else's life.

The answers you disclose are not meant for anyone to be judgmental. Your answers actually help create solutions that can be implemented for each individual's problems on a case-by-case basis.

Gangs

1. What set (gang) are you from?

2. If you're not a gang member, what gang do you run (hang) with?

3. How often do you hang with them?

4. Why do you hang with them?

5. What is your opinion about gang members?
   (paragraph)_____
   _____
   _____
   _____
   _____

6. How can you demonstrate that you do love yourself?

7. Do you love your family?

8. How can you become a positive member of society?

9. How can you bring positive value to your community? (paragraph)_____

_____

_____

_____

_____

10. What will give you the incentive to change your life? (paragraph)_____

_____

_____

_____

_____

11. Describe how gangs are bad for you, your family and community. (paragraph)_____

_____

_____

_____

_____

12. Write a list of all the people you know that died from gang violence.

_____

_____

_____

_____

_____

_____

13. Describe what you can do to prevent someone from joining a gang.(paragraph)_____

_____

_____

_____

_____

Drugs

1. What made you want to try drugs?

2. What drugs have you tried?

3. How often have you tried it?

4. How did it make you feel?

5. What is your drug of choice?

6. Name all the drugs you've ever tried.

7. What is the worst thing you ever did under the influence?

8. How has this drug stopped you from achieving your goals?

9. How many people do you know who have died from drug addiction?

10. What are the things you can do to better yourself? (paragraph)

_____

_____

_____

_____

_____

11. How can you become an asset to your family and community? (paragraph)

_____

_____

_____

_____

_____

Alcohol

1. What made you want to try alcohol?

2. How often do you drink?

3. What is your drink of choice?

4. What is the worst thing you've ever done under the influence of alcohol?

5. How has alcohol stopped you from achieving your goals?

6. How many people do you know of that have died because of alcohol?

7. How many people have you hurt while under the influence of alcohol?

8. Have you had any DUI's (Driving under the Influence) arrest?

9. What are some of the benefits of living sober? (paragraph)

_____

_____

_____

_____

_____

10. Living sober, how can you become an asset to your family and community?
(paragraph)_____

_____

_____

_____

_____

Family

1. How has your behavior affected your family? (paragraph)

   _____

   _____

   _____

   _____

   _____

2. Do you acknowledge the pain that you have caused your family?

3. If you have siblings or younger family members, do you want them to be like you?

4. Have you been hurt by a family member?

5. Do you feel you have your family's support to live a positive life?

6. If you had to change one thing about yourself what would it be?

7. If you could change one thing about your family, what would it be?

8. Do you feel you are strong enough to make the changes necessary to start a new life?

9. Do you know how to go about bettering your life?

10. If you could change one thing about yourself, what would it be? (paragraph)_____

_____

_____

_____

_____

Future

1. What do you desire to become in life?

2. Have you started to pursue or reach this goal?

3. What is stopping you from pursuing your goals?

4. What resources do you need to reach your goals?

5. Is there anyone in your life that can help you reach your goals?

6. Would you like someone to help you to reach your goals?

7. How can you help save someone else today?

8. How can you do something every day to help someone else?

9. Who inspires you - and why?
    (paragraph)_____
    _____
    _____
    _____
    _____

7 Steps for Growth, Development and Transition...

(You have to complete each step, before you can move on to the next step)

1. REPENTANCE

2. Ask yourself for FORGIVENESS and anyone you may have hurt or caused pain.

3. Move FORWARD and let go of the past.

4. Create a vision board of GOALS, and set a goal chart for 30 DAYS; every Saturday, review your progress.

5. Create a 90-day GOAL chart; every Saturday, review your progress.

6. Create a 1 year VISION BOARD of goals; every Saturday review your progress

Write (7) seven things that you are GRATEFUL for._____

_____
_____
_____
_____
_____

My Notes:

Order Form

Total Solidarity Publishing, LLC

3717 S. LaBrea Ave, Suite 197
Los Angeles, CA 90016
Phone (323) 602-4273
www.totalsolidaritypublishing.com

Customer Information:
Name: _____

Shipping Address: _____

City: _____ **State:** _____ **Zip Code:** _____

Phone: (____)_____

**Payment must accompany order request **
Email Address: _____

Order Information

Today's Date: _____

Type of Media   **Quantity**   **Total**

SINGLE CD ($6.00 each)   _____qty. $_____ *

PAPERBACK ($14.00 each)   _____qty. $_____ *

*Shipping & Handling Included

E-books can be purchased at www.totalsolidaritypublishing.com

---

Method of Payment
☐ **Money Order:**
☐ **Credit Card: May be purchased via telephone 323-602-4273**
☐ **Check (No._____)**
(*Please make check payable to Total Solidarity Publishing, LLC.*)

Check Info:

Driver's License Number:_____

Expiration Date:_____

(Returned checks are subject to additional processing fees)

---

www.ingramcontent.com/pod-product-compliance
Lightning Source LLC
LaVergne TN
LVHW021610080426
835510LV00019B/2502